Contents

1

Oceanic whitetip shark *(Carcharhinus longimanus)*

Sharks

There are no villains in the sea, but danger still exists.
In the common quest of all creatures to reproduce, feed
and survive, the myriad species of sea life have evolved
a formidable array of protective mechanisms. There are
biters, stingers, poisoners and shockers. Most dangerous
sea creatures are passive in nature and do not seek out
man. Sharks, among the topmost marine predators,
present the greatest threat.

Lords of the sea

All sharks are carnivorous and many are potentially dangerous to man. There are more than 250 species, ranging from sharks that mature at about one foot, to the largest of all fishes, the whale shark, known to reach a length of 45 feet. While the whale shark and another large species, the basking shark, feed on plankton and therefore pose no real threat to man, other large sharks must remain suspect.

Sharks are elasmobranchs, having a skeletal structure made up of cartilage, which has left few complete fossils. Fossils that do remain show little change in body form through the ages. Their efficient torpedolike shape is still typical of most sharks. They are incredibly well adapted. These tireless prowlers of all oceans and some rivers have few enemies save each other.

Very little is known about sharks in their natural habitat. Research in the field is extremely difficult. Though sharks have survived hundreds of millions of years of change and upheaval in the marine world, they are very fragile in captivity. They often die from shock, or refuse to feed. Most large sharks are solitary by nature, but congregations of **silky sharks** (*Carcharhinus falciformis, below*) are sometimes seen far from shore.

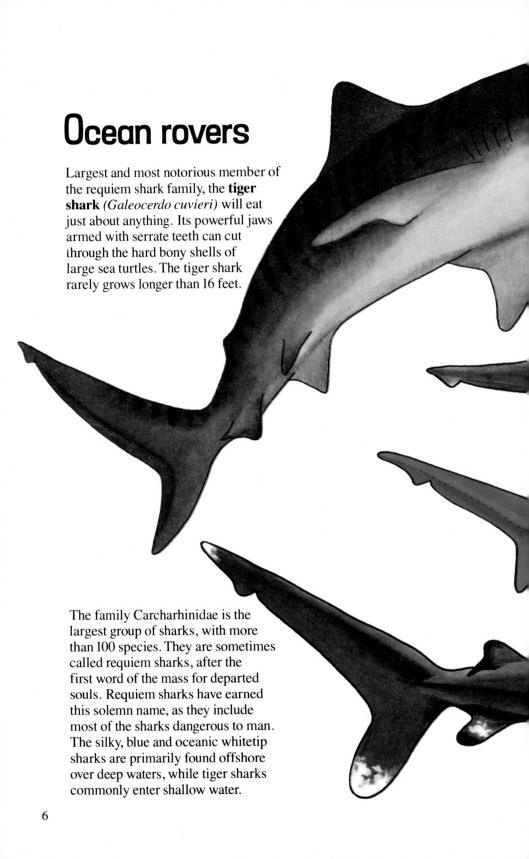

Ocean rovers

Largest and most notorious member of
the requiem shark family, the **tiger
shark** *(Galeocerdo cuvieri)* will eat
just about anything. Its powerful jaws
armed with serrate teeth can cut
through the hard bony shells of
large sea turtles. The tiger shark
rarely grows longer than 16 feet.

The family Carcharhinidae is the
largest group of sharks, with more
than 100 species. They are sometimes
called requiem sharks, after the
first word of the mass for departed
souls. Requiem sharks have earned
this solemn name, as they include
most of the sharks dangerous to man.
The silky, blue and oceanic whitetip
sharks are primarily found offshore
over deep waters, while tiger sharks
commonly enter shallow water.

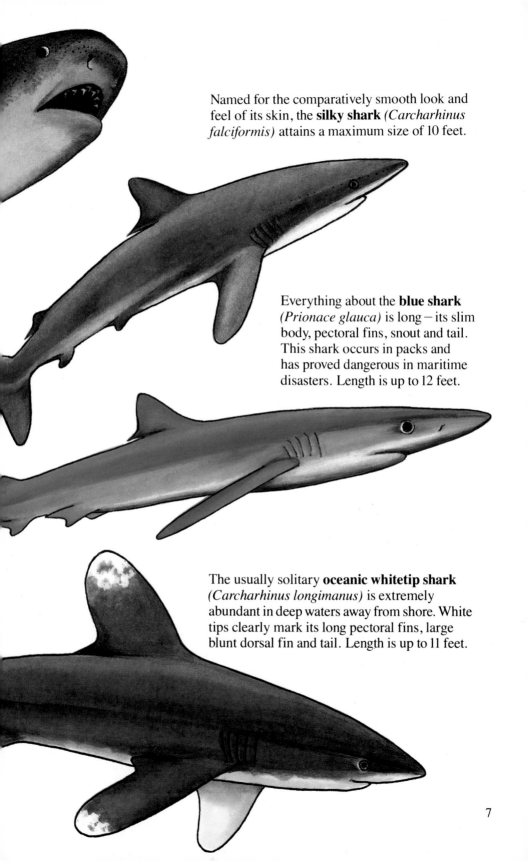

Named for the comparatively smooth look and feel of its skin, the **silky shark** *(Carcharhinus falciformis)* attains a maximum size of 10 feet.

Everything about the **blue shark** *(Prionace glauca)* is long – its slim body, pectoral fins, snout and tail. This shark occurs in packs and has proved dangerous in maritime disasters. Length is up to 12 feet.

The usually solitary **oceanic whitetip shark** *(Carcharhinus longimanus)* is extremely abundant in deep waters away from shore. White tips clearly mark its long pectoral fins, large blunt dorsal fin and tail. Length is up to 11 feet.

7

The **oceanic whitetip shark** *(Carcharhinus longimanus)*
presents a heavily rounded body terminating in a short,
broad snout as it lumbers through warm ocean waters.
Longimanus, Latin for "long hand," describes the oversized
pectoral fins. Though slow-moving and lethargic in appearance, the whitetip prevails over all other sharks in its
domain, not only in size and aggressiveness, but also in
sheer numbers. It may be the most abundant large animal
in the oceans. Luckily, it is not found close to shore,
and presents little danger to most swimmers or divers.

Bull shark *(Carcharhinus leucas)*
A potential danger to swimmers, the bull shark frequents inshore waters and enters rivers. A broadly rounded snout and heavy, robust body distinguish this shark. The bull shark may grow to ten feet.

Lemon shark *(Negaprion brevirostris)*
This slim-bodied shark has a second dorsal fin almost as large as the first. The lemon is found in inshore waters. Like most sharks, its color varies, but the lemon shark is usually a shade of yellowish brown. Length is up to 12 feet.

Nurse shark *(Ginglymostoma cirratum)*
This shark grows to 14 feet, and has a distinctive tail lacking an extended lower lobe. It is the only coastal Atlantic shark with barbels. Found most often in shallow water, it may at times lie motionless on the bottom. Many divers have been tempted to tweak its tail or otherwise molest the nurse shark. Such actions may account for injuries inflicted on divers by these generally non-aggressive sharks.

Blacktip shark *(Carcharhinus limbatus)*
A long-snouted coastal shark, the blacktip is aptly named for the dark markings tipping some of its fins. This fast-swimming shark is often seen jumping from the water. Maximum size is eight feet.

Sand tiger *(Odontaspis taurus)*
The young and some adults of this species are marked with irregular spots or blotches. They have two equal-sized dorsal fins and reach a maximum length of nine feet.

Reef
roamers

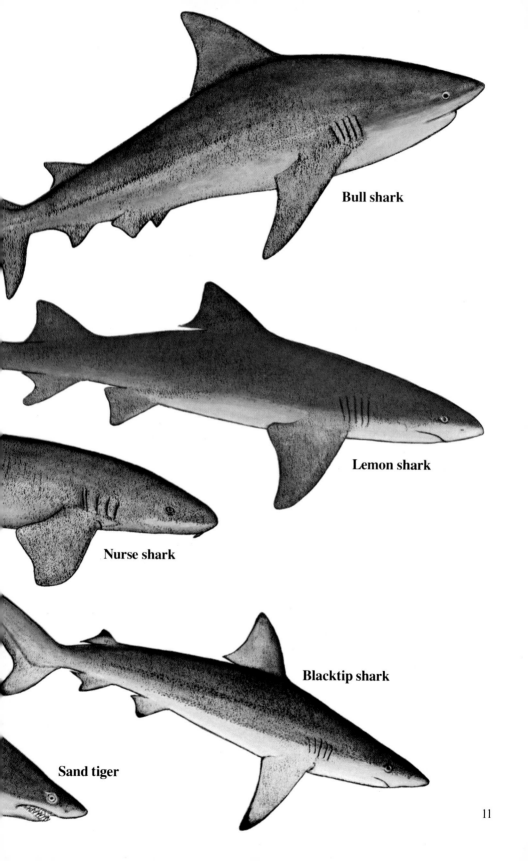

Bull shark

Lemon shark

Nurse shark

Blacktip shark

Sand tiger

11

The shark most likely to be encountered by the greatest
number of people is the **bull shark** *(Carcharhinus leucas)*.
It inhabits fresh and saltwater rivers and oceans, and
is rarely far from shore. The bull shark is found in the
Pacific and Indian oceans and on both sides of the Atlantic
as well. It has poked its way upriver in the Mississippi,
Zambezi, Amazon, Euphrates, Tigris, Ganges and into Lake
Nicaragua. The bull shark was thought to be a separate
species in each locale until recently. Known in South
Africa as the Zambezi shark, it is one of the creatures
that has terrorized the Natal Coast.

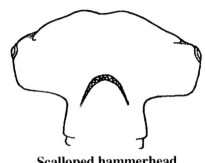

Scalloped hammerhead

Hammerheads

The shark family Sphyrnidae, comprising the hammerheads, is the most readily identified of all groups. For no proven function, the eyes and nostrils are located at the tips of the lateral lobes of the head. Variations in the shape of the head help to differentiate among species. There have been several well-authenticated attacks on man by these powerful swimmers. While they normally eat stingrays and other fishes, specimens have been found with such diverse objects as beer cans and other hammerheads in their stomachs.

Scalloped hammerhead *(Sphyrna lewini)* Pectoral fins are tipped with black on this gray shark. Maximum length is about 12 feet.

Smooth hammerhead *(Sphyrna zygaena)* Bronze with dusky fin tips, the smooth hammerhead may grow to 13 feet.

Great hammerhead *(Sphyrna mokarran)* Attaining a length of possibly 18 feet, this is the largest and most dangerous hammerhead.

Bonnethead *(Sphyrna tiburo)* With a head shaped more like a shovel than a hammer, the bonnethead rarely grows more than four feet long. This shark is commonly seen inshore.

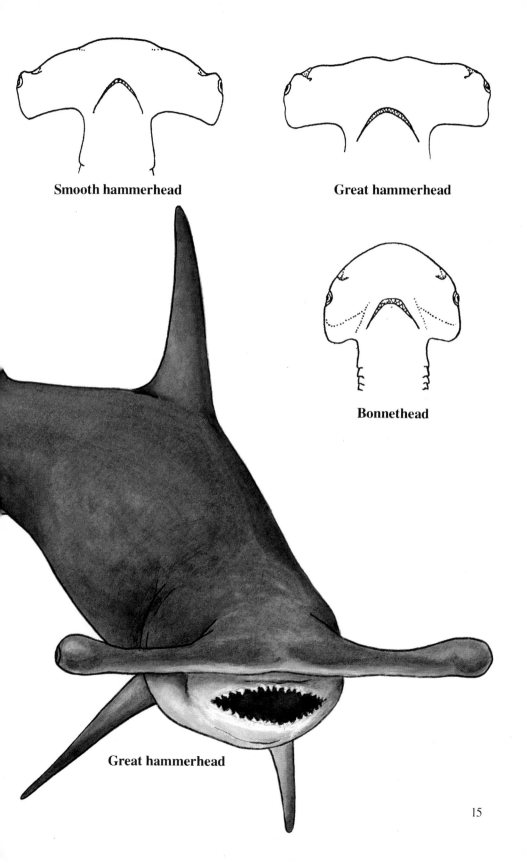

Smooth hammerhead

Great hammerhead

Bonnethead

Great hammerhead

15

Great hammerhead

The **great white shark** *(Carcharodon carcharias, top),* also called man-eater, is not found in abundance anywhere, yet it has been implicated in more attacks upon man than any other shark. Its normal diet includes large mammals such as sea lions. This swift, powerful, most voracious of sharks is known to attack even boats without provocation.

The young are over 100 pounds at birth. Mature great white sharks are known to reach 20 feet, and can weigh 6000 pounds at that length. The great white and the **shortfin mako** *(Isurus oxyrhinchus, bottom)* are members of the Lamnidae, or mackerel shark family. The mako is much smaller and lighter-bodied than the great white, but both can be recognized by their lunate tail and pointed snout. The mako is the only shark swift enough to feed on swordfish and mackerel, and the only shark listed as a salt water sportsman's game fish.

Mighty mackerel sharks

Great white shark

Shortfin mako

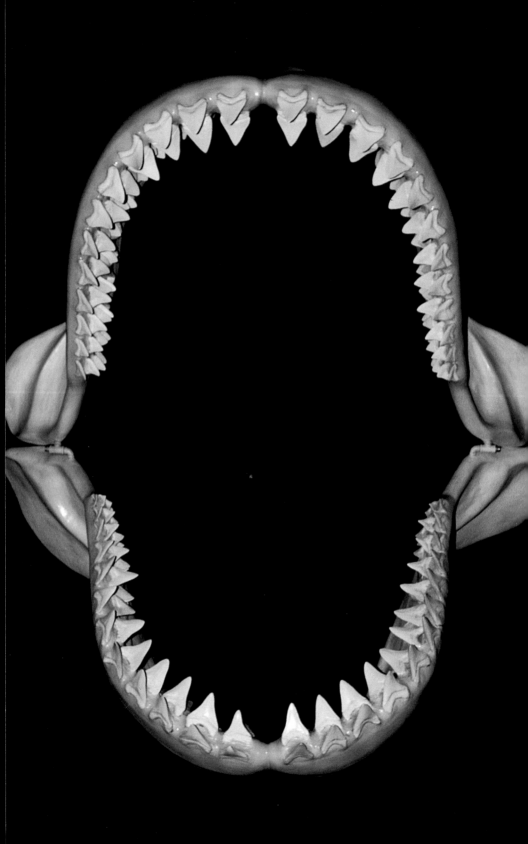

Jaws

Fossil records of early sharks are based for the most part on their teeth. The reconstructed jaw of the **giant white shark** *(Carcharodon megalodon, left)* opens wide enough to accommodate an object 3.5 x 5 feet. This now-extinct species is believed to have reached a length of 45 feet during the Miocene era, 30 to 60 million years ago. Giant white shark teeth have been found up to five inches long. The present-day great white shark *(Carcharodon carcharias)* closely resembles this ancient species. Its estimated maximum size of over 20 feet is based on authenticated specimen teeth 2.5 inches long.

One way to identify a shark is by its teeth. They are usually sharp, pointed and serrate, excellent for holding and cutting. Sharks have 5 to 15 rows of teeth in reserve. New teeth are constantly moving forward to replace missing teeth. Generally, when the shark is feeding, it grabs prey between its powerful jaws and uses a fierce shaking motion to bite off massive chunks.

Tests at the Mote Marine Laboratory utilized a unique device to determine the power of a shark's bite. The "bite-meter," an aluminum core of specific hardness in a specially designed casing, was camouflaged within a bait fish. When the shark bit, the force dented the aluminum core. The bite exerted by the 8-foot **dusky shark** *(Carcharhinus obscurus, above)* was estimated by Dr. Perry W. Gilbert at approximately 18 tons per square inch.

Peerless
predators

This **lemon shark**, after an exploratory circle or two, grabbed the dead bait fish. When a speared or wounded fish is alive and still struggling, a shark may move in with less hesitation and attack immediately. One hammerhead was observed to be in such haste to devour a meal that it snatched the fish and impaled itself upon the spear. Undaunted, it continued to feed and then, spear still in its mouth and protruding through the gills, swam off.

Though they will often feed on targets of opportunity such as the weak and disabled, sharks are predators, and can easily pursue and capture healthy prey. The diet, varying with each species, includes fishes, crabs, sea urchins, rays, seals and sea turtles.

Sharks have the ability to open their jaws widely, actually dislocating the upper jaw, and can swallow large prey in one gulp. A tiger shark weighing 900 pounds was found to have consumed, whole, a 200 pound hammerhead. Cannibalism among sharks has been well documented. Attempts to capture sharks alive are often foiled by other sharks that eat their hooked brothers. In a feeding frenzy, sharks have been filmed snapping at anything they encounter, including each other.

Sight research

In the past, it was believed sharks had poor eyesight. Scientific studies have proved otherwise. Dr. Samuel H. Gruber *(left)* describes one of a series of experiments based on classical conditioning to determine just what a shark sees. Lemon sharks were used because they are hardy and survive best in captivity.

"Similar to Pavlov's dogs," notes Dr. Gruber, "the lemon sharks responded to minimal, low-voltage electric shocks by 'blinking' a third eyelid, or nictitating membrane *(below)*. A flash of light and a shock were paired until the shark blinked when it saw a flash. The changes in sensitivity as the shark's eye adjusted to darkness were measured. The shark was actually being asked: 'Do you see this flash of light?' The shark replied 'yes' if it blinked and 'no' if the nictitating membrane did not move. The rate of dark adaptation was slower than humans tested on the same apparatus, but the final sensitivity of the shark was ten times greater. This indicates shark eyes are more sensitive to light than human eyes. In favorable conditions, sharks probably can hunt visually by moonlight and possibly by starlight!"

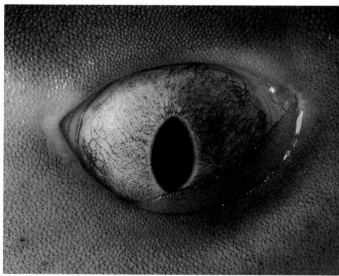

Sight, smell and sound research

One reason why sharks can see in very dim light is that the shark eye has thousands of little mirrors to reflect existing light back onto the retina. When the light level is too bright, pigment cells send down "shades" to cover these mirrors. In addition, the pupil in a shark's eye dilates and contracts with light, unlike that of most other fishes. Because of these mechanisms, it is now believed sharks are not exclusively nocturnal, but rather that they are able to feed day and night, at will.

In classic experiments on the learning ability of sharks, Dr. Eugenie Clark established that sharks could be taught to distinguish patterns utilized on targets. Research continues to determine if sharks can see color, or are reacting to the brightness or intensity of colors. Dr. Duco Hamasaki *(right)* studies the electrical activity of a shark's retina, looking for mechanisms of color response.

It is certain that sharks rely on sight when close to prey, but beyond their visual limits, the sense of smell is dominant. Sharks can follow a trail of scent even when prey is not visible. They do not depend only on the smell of blood, but are attracted to "fish juice," a secretion given off by fish in distress.

For long-range location of prey, sharks depend on sound detection. Lemon sharks can hear low-frequency vibrations, from 10 to about 800 cycles per second. This is within the range of sounds made by struggling or wounded fish. Proof that sharks are attracted by these sounds was obtained when the vibrations were recorded and played back underwater. Dr. Arthur Myrberg found that these recordings drew sharks from as far away as 900 feet. Sharks home in on these sounds with their extremely sensitive vibration detectors, the inner ear and lateral line system. The latter is a highly developed sensory network extending along the body and face.

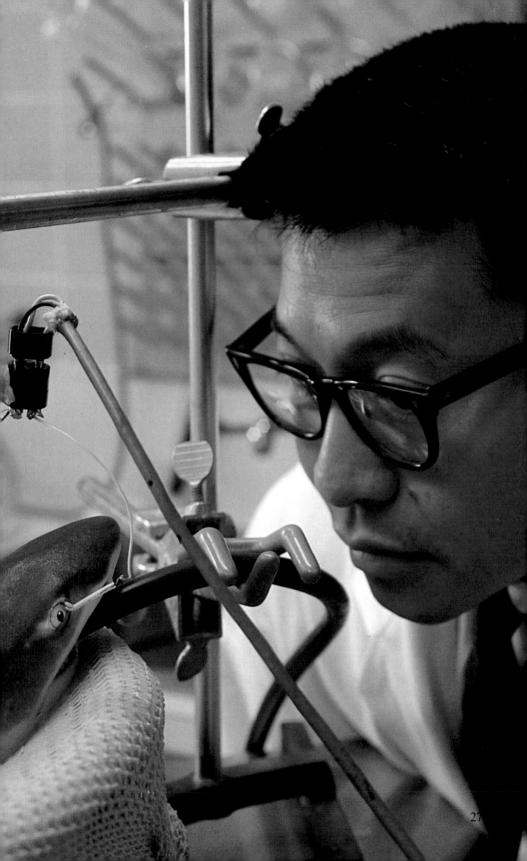

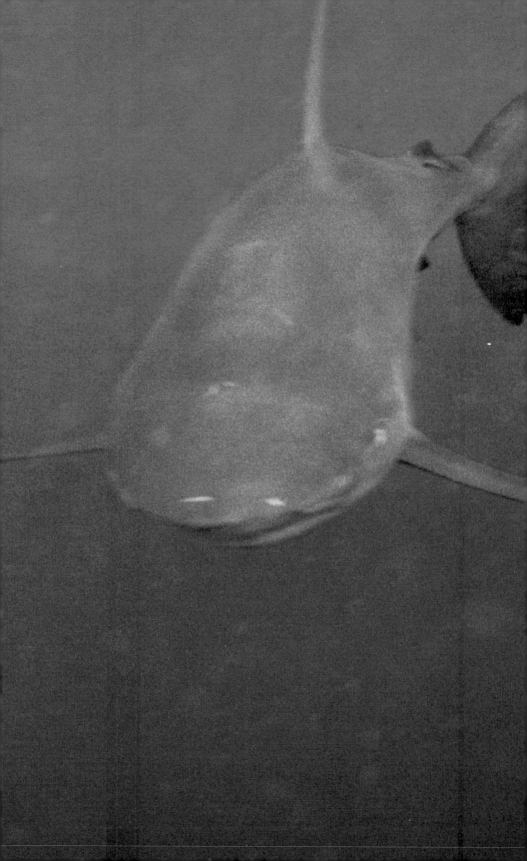

Attack!

A head-on confrontation with a man-eating shark is a universal primeval fear. Like most fears, it is highly exaggerated. More people are struck by lightning in the United States alone than are attacked by sharks worldwide in an average year. Of the small number who are attacked, about 75 percent of present-day victims survive. Considering the expanding use of beaches for recreational activities (where most attacks take place), the odds against being attacked take on a more realistic perspective.

However, some cases parallel the fictional nightmares detailed in pulp magazines and exploitation films. Tim Wallett's book, "Shark Attack," is a study of the Natal Coast of South Africa, the shark-attack capital of the world. In one case history, two teenagers are described swimming from shore towards a yacht. Halfway there, one of the boys paused to do a comic imitation of the female victim's struggles in the film, "Jaws." Minutes later, he was attacked by a shark, most likely a great white. His chest was grasped in a single bite of the jaw and then let go. Fortunately, he survived with superficial wounds.

Many aspects of this incident are typical of other attacks. The victim was swimming apart from his buddy. The mimic struggle, suggesting a creature in distress, apparently created some provocation. There was no further attack, even though blood was present in the water and the shark was sighted again. The other person in the water was unharmed. The attack took place at a popular beach area known for other such incidents. Lastly, it occurred during what Dr. H. Baldridge calls "shark attack season," that time of year when the water is warm enough for people and not too hot for sharks (70°-85° F). During this time, there is maximum exposure of people to sharks, affording greater opportunity for attacks.

Photographer Jerry Greenberg, on assignment for National Geographic magazine, and shark specialist Dr. Donald Nelson shared lunch with this six-foot **silky shark**, hand-feeding it from the side of their boat. When they later entered the water, the silky attacked with such speed that Nelson, armed with a 12-gauge bangstick, barely had time to

push the shark off. Greenberg desperately maneuvered himself out of
the way after taking this dramatic picture. Nelson killed the silky
on its next charge. This attack was undoubtedly provoked by the
feeding, and was one of the rare circumstances when either of the
divers had to destroy a shark in self-defense.

The **oceanic whitetip** *(Carcharhinus longimanus)* dominates warm surface waters of open oceans throughout the world. It rarely, if ever, approaches shore, posing no danger to coastal swimmers. However, large congregations of oceanic whitetips have been seen at the sites of mid-ocean disasters, and they are believed to be a major threat to survivors.

Man and shark

The growing popularity of skindiving in recent years has led to a greater proximity of man and shark than ever before. Almost every skindiver has a shark story, and most live to tell the tale. Despite the deeply held belief by divers that they are not prone to attack, about one of every three shark attack victims is a diver. Many of these cases were the direct result of a diver overtly molesting a shark. In more than half the cases, spearfishing was involved. Fish in distress give off "juices" and vibrations that attract sharks from considerable distances.

Though not immune to attack, divers have sustained comparatively slight injuries, and had a high rate of survival. Most diver-victims were apart from a group, but had potential rescuers nearby, some of whom actively fought the shark off. While spearfishing may have inadvertently brought on the initial attack, the availability of a weapon with which to engage the shark may account for the lower incidence of serious injuries. Spearguns have been most effective when used as a shark billy, to fend off the attacker.

Sharks will attack all races and nationalities. There is not total equality, however. Shark attack files as a whole indicate a ratio of over thirteen males attacked for each female. Among divers, the ratio as of 1973 was 243 males to one female.

In case of attack...

Carry the victim out of water in a head-down position. Place the victim, still head-down to minimize bleeding, on a towel or blanket, legs elevated. Do not remove wetsuit or apparel. Stop bleeding immediately either by direct hand pressure on the wound or packing with a pressure pad. Reassure the victim continuously. It is preferable to bring medical assistance to the victim on the site. Do not move the victim until the circulatory system is stabilized.

One safe way to observe and photograph sharks
is from a protective cage, such as this one
designed and manned by engineer J.G. Stemples.
Tethered to a boat in the shark-infested waters
of Tongue of the Ocean, Bahamas, it dangles
15 feet below the surface. Pieces of herring
dispensed from a bag bring a pack of aggressive
silky sharks within camera range. One silky
managed to wedge itself halfway inside the cage
and was summarily kicked out. Other silkies
taste-tested free-swimming photographer Jerry
Greenberg's fins and light meter.

Shark sense

- Don't swim or dive alone. There is safety in numbers. Help is at hand if you have someone with you.
- Stay out of the water if sharks are known to be in the area.
- Don't swim if menstruating or with a bleeding injury.
- Boat all speared fish immediately. Never spearfish continuously in a limited area or carry speared fish on your person.
- Do not provoke, molest or spear any shark, no matter how small or harmless a species appears to be.
- Avoid swimming in dirty water, at dusk, or at night.
- Sharks have a predilection for attacking bright, contrasty or reflective objects. Avoid wearing or carrying such objects.
- Don't swim or dive where garbage or human waste is dumped.

If you sight a shark, don't panic. Leave the water as soon as possible. Swim away, preferably underwater, with a smooth, rhythmic stroke. Keep sight of the shark. If it moves in, fend it off with a stick, try to probe the eyes, gills or nose, or hit it on the snout with the heaviest instrument available. Use your fist only as a last resort, for the shark's skin is rough and will cause bleeding. Make some defensive effort. Attack files list many instances when the victim acted successfully in defense.

These rules are based on information from the Shark Research Panel funded by the U.S. Navy. The panel consisted of such experts as Perry Gilbert, Leonard Schultz, Albert Tester and Stewart Springer. Another source of information was the report "Shark Attack Against Man," a computerized analysis of the Shark Attack File by Captain H. David Baldridge, also sponsored by the U.S. Navy.

Other dangerous sea creatures

Spotted eagle ray

Rays

Rays vary in form from an almost
perfect diamond shape to a disk.
Though often seen lying motionless on
the bottom partly buried in sand, they are strong
swimmers, propelled by graceful undulations of their
winglike pectoral fins. The mouth and gill slits are on the
underside of the body, with the eyes on the upper side.
A pair of large openings behind the eyes enables most rays to
draw in water for breathing without having to open the mouth.
Stingrays have a serrated spine on the upper surface of the tail
base, which is venomous. If stabbed by this spine, remove
particles. Irrigate the wound with salt water, and then soak in
hot water. Disinfect and seek medical help. Unless stepped on
or otherwise molested, rays are harmless.

Southern stingray

Spotted eagle ray *(Aetobatus narinari)*
This large ray (up to eight feet
long) has a well-defined head
set off from its pectoral fins. Like
the manta, this is an active ray.

Southern stingray *(Dasyatis americana)*
The winglike pectoral fins of this ray
extend forward to encompass the head.
A pale spot before the eyes marks
the five-foot-wide disk.

Atlantic manta *(Manta birostris)*
Mantas grow to a monstrous size of
over 20 feet and 3000 pounds. Also
called devilfish, they pose little
threat to man. Unlike other rays, the
mouth is in front. Limblike flaps
project from the head forward of the
eyes. Mantas swim with mouth open,
straining food from the water.

Smalltooth sawfish *(Pristis pectinata)*
Sweeping through schools of small fish,
this sharklike ray feeds by slashing
with its tooth-edged saw. The
smalltooth sawfish reaches 20 feet.

Yellow stingray *(Urolophus jamaicensis)*
Though small, with a mottled disk no
wider than 15 inches, the yellow
stingray can inflict pain from its spine
if stepped on or carelessly handled.

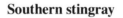

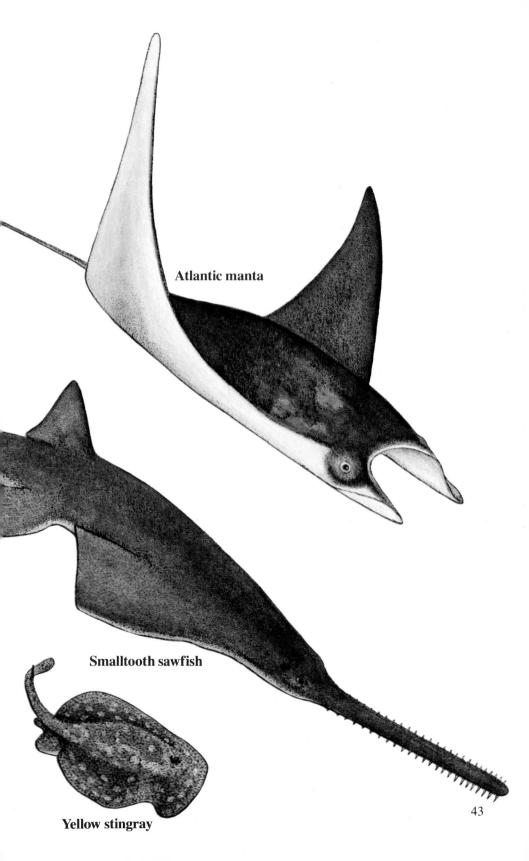

Atlantic manta

Smalltooth sawfish

Yellow stingray

43

Stinging corals

All corals can inflict slow-healing wounds on skin, but none causes as much pain as stinging corals. Distant relatives of stony corals, they may vary in form from a flat encrusting growth to branching or leaflike structures. Polyps are very small and do not form visible cups, lending these corals a smoother looking surface than other corals. **Encrusting stinging coral** (*Millepora alcicornis, left*) forms branching colonies. **Leafy stinging coral** (*Millepora complanata, right*) often grows facing wave direction. After contact, apply alcohol or other antiseptic.

Portuguese man-o-war

Threadlike tentacles dangle from the gas-filled float of the **Portuguese man-of-war** *(Physalia physalis, right)*. Each tentacle has stinging cells capable of causing extreme pain, shock, or even respiratory paralysis. The balloonlike float on a colony may exceed six inches, with tentacles trailing to 60 feet. The float is harmless, but the tentacles can sting even when the colony is washed ashore, and should never be handled or stepped on. If stung, remove all adhering material, taking care not to expose skin to further stinging. Apply shaving cream and shave with a safety razor. Toxin in the blood stream will still be active. If symptoms are severe, consult a doctor.

Sea urchin

The **long-spined sea urchin** *(Diadema antillarum, below)* has a brittle, domed shell with movable, projecting spines. If stepped on or handled, these barbed spines break off under the skin and become firmly embedded. Swelling and pain may follow for several hours. If stung, remove as many fragments as possible and apply ammonia or antiseptic. The shell, or test, may reach four inches across, with spines up to 16 inches long.

Jellyfish

Jellyfish are not fish at all, but a more primitive organism related to corals. Rhythmic contractions propel jellyfish, though heavy tides or wave action may wash them ashore. All jellyfish have pendant tentacles with minute stinging organs that enable them to stun the small forms of life they feed on. These tentacles can cause pain on contact with skin. Avoid rubbing injured areas, as this may activate additional stingers. Do not touch with bare hands. The best treatment is to apply shaving cream and shave with a safety razor. Follow with an application of meat tenderizer on moistened skin. Allow this solution to remain until irritation is gone, and then rinse off with water.

The **upside-down jellyfish** *(Cassiopeia xamachana, right),* shown here in an upright, free-swimming phase, normally rests inverted on the sea bottom in stagnant, shallow water. The disk is usually dome-shaped, and may grow to one foot in diameter. Generally harmless, Cassiopeia can inflict a painful sting if rudely disrupted.

The **moon jellyfish** *(Aurelia aurita, below)* has a transparent, fleshy disk fringed with pale tentacles that can cause temporary burning on contact. Disk size may exceed one foot.

Bristle worm

White-tipped bristles are a form of armament for the **bristle worm** *(Eurythöe complanata or Hermodice carunculata, top right)*. These brittle lengths of glasslike matter detach easily on contact with skin, producing severe pain for several hours. If affected, do not rub. Remove imbedded bristles with tweezers and apply alcohol or ammonia. Size is about 8 inches. Color may be orange or green.

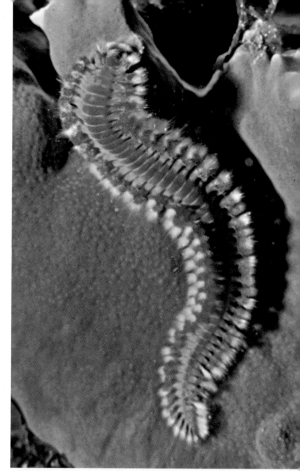

Fire sponges

Red fire sponge *(Tedania ignis, lower right)* is generally found in grass flats, bays and lagoons. It may occur in a variety of shapes, with colonies 4 to 12 inches high. When touched, it causes itching, swelling, and pain similar to a bad case of poison ivy. Another species of fire sponge, the "do-not-touch-me sponge" *(Neofibularia nolitangere)*, produces a severe sting. This dull mahogany-colored sponge may often be found in deeper waters growing among corals. The **red wall sponge** *(Haliclona compressa)* and the **orange sponge** *(Agelas sp., left)* growing alongside are harmless, but the wise reefcomber will wear gloves and avoid touching red or orange sponges. Treat affected areas with dilute vinegar or antiseptic.

51

Scorpionfish

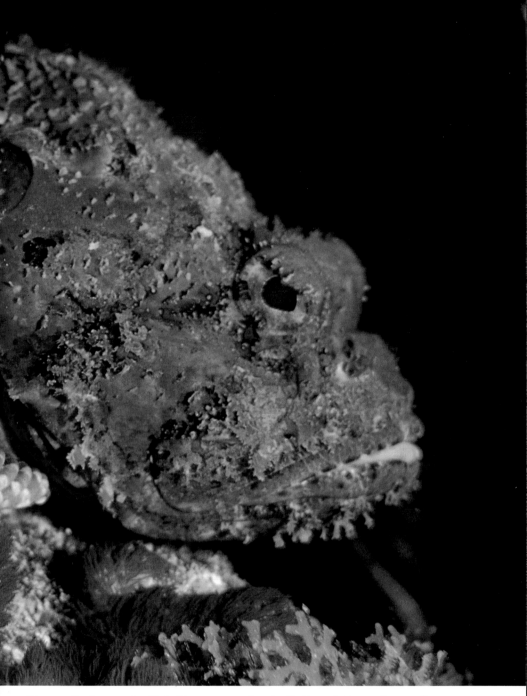

The **spotted scorpionfish** *(Scorpaena plumieri)* sits quietly on the sea floor, preying on small creatures that venture near its well-camouflaged exterior. This species of scorpionfish may reach a length of 18 inches. When touched or stepped on, wounds from its spines cause infection and great pain. If stung, remove any remaining particles. Wash the wound in sea water, and then soak in hot water. Consult a doctor.

Goldentail morays

Morays

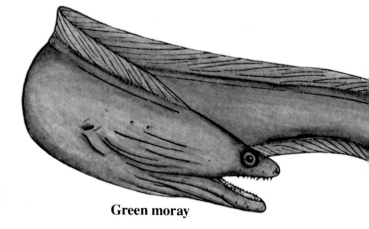

Green moray

Green moray *(Gymnothorax funebris)*
This species reaches the greatest size of Atlantic morays, more than six feet. The green color is the result of a yellowish mucus overlaying the dark blue skin.

Goldentail moray *(Muraena miliaris)*
A small eel not exceeding two feet, the goldentail moray has tiny teeth, even for its size. The attractive yellow markings vary greatly, but the golden color is most extensive and pronounced at the tail tip.

Spotted moray *(Gymnothorax moringa)*
This moray is usually found in shallow-water coral and rock areas. It may grow to four feet.

Viper moray *(Enchelycore nigricans)*
Strongly arched jaws expose the many awesome teeth of the viper moray, even when the mouth is closed. This eel ranges up to three feet long.

Purplemouth moray *(Gymnothorax vicinus)* Varying in body color from a nearly uniform brown to a densely-mottled pattern, the purplemouth may grow to four feet. The dark purplish color inside the lower jaw contrasts with pale lavender at the roof.

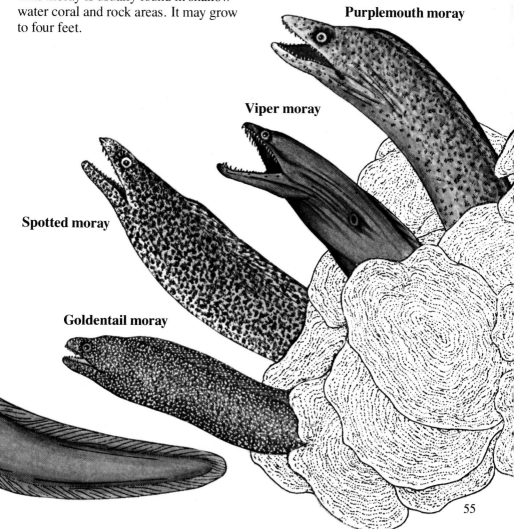

Purplemouth moray

Viper moray

Spotted moray

Goldentail moray

55

The **spotted moray** (*Gymnothorax moringa, above*) may be very aggressive in defending its territory. The **goldentail moray** (*Muraena miliaris, left*) is the most commonly seen moray on Florida reefs.

As beautiful and repulsive as the snakes they resemble, these fish have smooth, scaleless skin. Largely nocturnal and secretive by nature, morays hide in crevices and under coral ledges. They are generally harmless to man unless provoked. Narrow, muscular jaws can drive the fanglike teeth deeply into anything they grasp. The bite itself is not toxic, but since the teeth are invariably covered with slime, serious infection may follow if the wound is not treated. Clean and disinfect the wound. See a doctor. Morays should never be eaten, since some individuals of many species can cause severe food poisoning, and even death.

Barracuda—
tiger of the sea

Armed with long, razor-sharp teeth and capable of speeds up to 27 mph, the **great barracuda** *(Sphyraena barracuda)* is a formidable hunter. Though guilty of some attacks on man, people are not its natural prey.

Barracudas rely on keen eyesight to locate food, and in turbid water may mistake the flash of a bracelet or flutter of a foot for the mainstay of their diet, fish. Barracudas slash their prey in one pass of concentrated ferocity, swallowing small fish whole or returning for pieces of larger fish. The bite is distinctive, with two straight, almost parallel lines of toothmarks.

Though the great barracuda may reach six feet and over 100 pounds, it is unlikely to attack anything as large as a human for food. Most documented attacks have occurred in murky, shallow water as bathers were splashing in the surf. Wounds are usually superficial, and result in few fatalities.

Divers are often followed by curious barracudas for hours, without incident. Experienced divers stay out of dirty water, avoid shiny jewelry or equipment, and do not spearfish when barracudas are present. That may account for the rarity of barracuda attacks on divers.

People on boats should not trail hands or feet in the water, and must take care when gutting and rinsing fish over the side. In case of an attack, clean and disinfect the wound, try to control bleeding, treat for shock, and summon medical aid immediately.

Experts agree that of the 20 species worldwide, only one, the great barracuda, poses a threat to man. They also agree the danger from attack is minuscule compared to that of contracting tropical fish poisoning from eating barracuda.

Ciguatera—
tropical fish poisoning

The greatest danger from the sea may be on the dinner plate. Apart from bacterial contamination, which can be avoided by cleaning and icing fish immediately, there is a more virulent illness, called ciguatera, that may result from eating tropical reef fish. Even freshly caught and properly prepared fish can carry this disease.

Symptoms begin about 6 to 12 hours after ingestion. Diarrhea, nausea and stomach cramps are followed by neurological disturbances such as reversal of hot and cold sensations, dizziness, numbness in the mouth and extremities, skin rash, itching, general pain and muscle weakness. Severe poisoning may lead to paralysis and shock, with some cases ending in death. Ciguatera illness may last for several weeks or persist for up to 25 years. The average span of illness is six months, and the only treatment presently available is symptomatic.

Ciguatera toxins may originate in reef-dwelling microorganisms which are ingested by herbivorous fishes. Predators then eat these herbivores, acquiring the accumulated toxin from each fish. Fishes high on the predatory scale are most likely to have strong concentrations of toxin.

More than 400 species of fish worldwide have been linked to ciguatera. It is not possible to determine if any one fish is ciguatoxic except by a presently imperfect chemical assay of its flesh. Though certain species are more suspect than others, not all individuals of a species will be toxic. Fish caught on one side of an island may be toxic, while fish taken nearby from the other side may not.

Neither cooking nor freezing fish will destroy the toxin. Appearance or taste will not divulge the presence of toxin, and the folk test of feeding fish to the family cat is not reliable. There are some simple precautions to follow, however, that may drastically reduce the risk of suffering from ciguatera.

Rely on local fishermen for advice on edibility of fish. Never eat the internal organs of a fish, particularly the liver, where the highest concentration of toxins are found. Do not eat morays, barracuda, yellowfin or black groupers. Avoid eating large specimens of snapper, grouper, kingfish or amberjack. If you do eat any of these, individuals three pounds or less are usually safe.

Should you become ill, please report your case to Dr. Donald de Sylva, a fish ecologist in Florida who has researched ciguatera for over 20 years, at 305/350-7334. Go to the nearest hospital emergency room or call a physician.

Large individuals of **tiger grouper**
(Mycteroperca tigris) have been
linked to ciguatera poisoning.